Abschlussband A5

English G 21

Klassenarbeitstrainer
für Schülerinnen und Schüler

mit Audios und Lösungen
online

 Dein **Online-Angebot enthält:** Audios und Lösungen.

Dein Zugangscode auf
go.cornelsen.de | p6tn7-jofq7

English G 21 • Abschlussband A5 für die 5-jährige Sekundarstufe I

Klassenarbeitstrainer mit Lösungen und Lerntipps

Konzeption
Dr. Ursula Mulla und Nogi Mulla, Germering

Erarbeitet von
Martin Kohn, Frankfurt/Main
Bärbel Schweitzer, M.A., Staufen

In Zusammenarbeit mit der Englischredaktion
Dr. Christiane Kallenbach (Projektleitung)
Gwendolyn Düwel (verantwortliche Redakteurin), Ulrike Berendt
Susanne Bennetreu, Stefanie Juhnke (Bildredaktion)

Beratende Mitwirkung
Katrin Häntzschel, Wiesa

Tonaufnahmen
Clarity Studio Berlin

Illustrationen
Anne-Claire Martin, Berlin (S. 60); Constanze Schargan, Berlin (S. 6; 9; 10; 19)

Bildquellen
Alamy, Abingdon (S. 8: Oredia; S. 16: Daniel Templeton; S. 18: Alan King engraving; S. 26: mediablitzimages (uk) Limited; S. 31: Yadid Levy; S. 36: Ulrich Doering; S. 37: David Grossman; S. 41: Angela Hampton Picture; S. 52 Bild 1: Gari Wyn Williams, Bild 2: i4images rf, Bild 3: Carol Barrington, Bild 4: Howard Davies; S. 55: AlamyCelebrity); **Alice Springs School of the Air**, 80 Head Street, Alice Springs Northern Territory Australien, www.assoa.nt.edu.au (S. 14); **Cinetext**, Frankfurt/Main (S. 40: Allstar / Film 4); **Corbis**, Düsseldorf (S. 4 Mitte: Reuters / Darren Staples; S. 39: Demotix / JOE MWANGI; S. 52 Bild 5: JAI / Michele Falzone; S. 54 oben: Hans Neleman; S. 59: Ocean (RF)); **Getty Images**, München (S. 13: Sindre Ellingsen; S. 34: NY Daily News); **iStockphoto**, Calgary (S. 4 re.: Sara Winter, 2. v. li.: David Freund; S. 11: twobluedogs; S. 21: sturti; S. 24: londoneye; S. 33: tunart; S. 45: Michelle Malven; S. 46 li.: David Sucsy, re.: oneclearvision; S. 54 unten li.: drbimages); **Moritz Schweitzer**, Villingen-Schwenningen (S. 5); **Shutterstock**, New York (S. 4 li.: Taras Vyshnya, 2. v. re.: markrhiggins; S. 7 li.: Paul Coartney, re.: John Carnemolla; S. 23: stefanolunardi; S. 27: Minerva Studio; S. 29: Tracy Whiteside; S. 38: Dmitriy Shironosov; S. 46 Mitte: Goodluz; S. 49: Goodluz; S. 54 unten re.: Nejron Photo; S. 57: Monkey Business Images; S. 58: Poznyakov)

Textquellen
S. 14: Alice Springs School of the Air. From Alice Springs School of the Air, 80 Head Street, Alice Springs Northern Territory Australien, www.assoa.nt.edu.au; S. 61: FSJ in Hessen. From *Freiwilliges Soziales Jahr in Hessen*. http://www.fsj-hessen.de/global/show_document.asp?id=aaaaaaaaaaadmrj. Hessisches Sozialministerium

Hörtext
Track 8 (u. Lösungsheft S. 28): *Slumdog Millionaire: changing film-making in India.* Abridged and adapted from "How Slumdog Millionaire is changing film-making in India" by Paul MacInnes, Mumbai, 4 June 2009. http://www.guardian.co.uk/film/2009/jun/04/slumdog-millionaire-india (Stand 29.07.2009). Copyright Guardian News & Media Ltd 2009

Titelbild
iStockphoto, Calgary (Gewitterkind / Christopher Pattberg); **Corel Library** (flag Hintergund (M))

Layout und technische Umsetzung
Heike Freund, Hameln

Umschlaggestaltung
Klein und Halm Grafikdesign, Berlin

www.cornelsen.de
www.EnglishG.de

1. Auflage, 8. Druck 2025

© 2011 Cornelsen Verlag, Berlin
© 2018 Cornelsen Verlag GmbH, Mecklenburgische Str. 53, 14197 Berlin, E-Mail: service@cornelsen.de

Das Werk und seine Teile sind urheberrechtlich geschützt. Jede Nutzung in anderen als den gesetzlich zugelassenen Fällen bedarf der vorherigen schriftlichen Einwilligung des Verlages. Hinweis zu §§ 60 a, 60 b UrhG: Weder das Werk noch seine Teile dürfen ohne eine solche Einwilligung an Schulen oder in Unterrichts- und Lehrmedien (§ 60 b Abs. 3 UrhG) vervielfältigt, insbesondere kopiert oder eingescannt, verbreitet oder in ein Netzwerk eingestellt oder sonst öffentlich zugänglich gemacht oder wiedergegeben werden. Dies gilt auch für Intranets von Schulen und anderen Bildungseinrichtungen. Der Anbieter behält sich eine Nutzung der Inhalte für Text- und Data-Mining im Sinne § 44 b UrhG ausdrücklich vor. Soweit in diesem Lehrwerk Personen fotografisch abgebildet sind und ihnen von der Redaktion fiktive Namen, Berufe, Dialoge und Ähnliches zugeordnet oder diese Personen in bestimmte Kontexte gesetzt werden, dienen diese Zuordnungen und Darstellungen ausschließlich der Veranschaulichung und dem besseren Verständnis des Lehrwerksinhalts.

Druck: Athesiadruck GmbH, Bozen

ISBN 978-3-06-032316-6

INHALT

Unit	Klassenarbeit	Seite
Unit 1	**Klassenarbeit A** Listening • Mediation • Language • Mediation • Writing • Speaking	5
	Klassenarbeit B Reading • Language • Writing • Speaking	14
Unit 2	**Klassenarbeit A** Reading • Writing • Language • Study Skills • Speaking	20
	Klassenarbeit B Listening • Language • Mediation • Speaking	27
Unit 3	**Klassenarbeit A** Listening • Language • Writing • Speaking	34
	Klassenarbeit B Reading • Language • Mediation	41
Unit 4	**Klassenarbeit A** Listening • Language • Writing • Speaking	46
	Klassenarbeit B Reading • Language • Mediation	55
Zusatz	**Exam Skills** How to do well in a test	62

Schon wieder eine Klassenarbeit ...

Liebe Schülerin, lieber Schüler,
wer sich gut vorbereitet, kann der nächsten Klassenarbeit gelassen entgegenblicken. Der Klassenarbeitstrainer unterstützt dich ganz gezielt beim Üben für alle Klassenarbeiten. Du findest zu jeder Unit zwei Klassenarbeiten, mit denen du alle Fertigkeiten (skills) trainieren kannst, die du für die Klassenarbeiten benötigst.

Einige Tipps für ein erfolgreiches Lernen mit deinem Klassenarbeitstrainer:

Vorbereitung
Informiere dich genau über die Inhalte der kommenden Klassenarbeit. In einem Lernplan legst du fest, welche Aufgaben du an welchem Tag bearbeiten willst. Plane dazu genügend Zeit ein. Bei Unklarheiten solltest du zuerst im Englischbuch nachsehen. Erst wenn du hier nicht weiter kommst, holst du dir Hilfe von anderen. Am Tag vor der Arbeit wiederholst du nur kurz.

Inhaltsverzeichnis
Im Inhaltsverzeichnis kannst du ablesen, welche Kompetenzen pro Klassenarbeit geübt werden. Oft gibt es auch zwei unterschiedliche Aufgaben zu einer Kompetenz, z.B. zum Listening oder zum Writing. Wähle eine aus oder löse beide Aufgaben.

Lernheft
Führe ein Heft für Schreibaufgaben und zusätzliche Übungen. Achte auf Übersichtlichkeit (Datum, Überschrift, Aufgabe, Seite). Lege auf der ersten Seite ein Inhaltsverzeichnis an. So kannst du bei Unklarheiten immer wieder nachschlagen. Es hilft dir auch, wenn du eine Aufgabe wiederholen möchtest.

Lösungen
Die Lösungen zu allen Aufgaben findest du auf scook.de. Gib dazu den Zugangscode von Seite 1 ein. Vergleiche deine Lösungen mit den möglichen Lösungen. Sieh dir dabei deine Fehler ganz genau an und analysiere sie. Nur so kannst du aus deinen Fehlern lernen. In den Lösungen findest du Lerntipps mit weiteren Übungen und auch die Hörtexte.

Punkteschlüssel
Bei jeder Klassenarbeit ist die Gesamtpunktzahl für alle Aufgaben angegeben. Solltest du beim Lernen eigene Schwerpunkte setzen und deswegen Aufgaben weglassen, musst du die Gesamtpunktzahl neu ermitteln. Mit dem Punkteschlüssel kannst du deine Leistung einschätzen.

Übrigens: Die Klassenarbeiten in diesem Heft prüfen das Gelernte sehr ausführlich ab. Du brauchst daher für die Bearbeitung länger als eine Schulstunde.

Jetzt kann es aber wirklich losgehen – **let's get started!**

All the best,

Bärbel Schweitzer und Martin Kohn

Klassenarbeit A

Unit 1

5

Gesamtpunktzahl ohne Speaking _____ / 85   Note _____

Gesamtpunktzahl mit Speaking _____ / 101   Note _____

LISTENING   _____ / 19

🎧 01 **1   A high school photo competition**   _____ / 9

a) *Look at the photos, then listen to the discussion and write the correct number in the boxes. Explain your choice. (6P)*

☞ Falls du die Namen nicht gleich zuordnen kannst, mache dir Notizen dazu, was die Jury-Mitglieder über die Fotos sagen.

A

B

C

D

E

F

b) *Which picture would you give a prize to? Give reasons for your answer. (Three sentences) (3P)*

Unit 1 | Klassenarbeit A

🎧 02 2 An interview for the school radio station ___/ 10

a) *Listen to the radio interview and put the information about Maya in the correct order. (5P)*

	She was very excited when the art teacher announced her name.
	She started taking pictures ten years ago.
	She has already participated in a photo competition.
	Her best photographs show her family and friends.
	She thinks the light was very good.

b) *Listen again carefully. Then read the following sentences. Some of them are true, some of them are false. Tick the box and correct the false statements. (5P)*

Sentence	True	False	Correction
Maya started taking photos when she was five.	☐	☐	
She wasn't successful in her first competition.	☐	☐	
Maya planned to take a picture of her favourite kids' playground.	☐	☐	
Maya likes touristy photos very much.	☐	☐	
The prize is a very good camera.	☐	☐	

MEDIATION

___/9

A photo competition

The following text is taken from the Australian magazine 'The one and only Australia' which has started a photo competition.

'The one and only Australia' monthly photo competition

We love everything that's special, wonderful and unusual about Australia.
And we love seeing what you like about our country too. This month the topic of our photo competition is:

One moment in Sydney
Enter our competition and you could win a $500 camera!

How to enter:
When you've chosen your photo, write a short description of it.
You should also give details of when and where the photo was taken.

Some rules:
The closing date for your entries is October 10 at midnight.
The competition is open to anybody aged 16 and over.
You should send your name, your full address and telephone number and a caption.
Photos must be at least 1 MB in size.
Each person is allowed to hand in one photo only. Of course you can take part again next month!

E-mail your photo to:
photocompetition@theoneandonlyaustralia.au
Please note that letters (with photos) sent by post will not be accepted in the competition.

The winner:
The winner's photo will be published in our magazine next month together with his or her name.

Think you've got a winning photo? We're waiting to see it!

Einer deiner Freunde ist ein guter Fotograf und möchte an diesem Wettbewerb teilnehmen. Hilf ihm, den Text zu verstehen. Schreibe deine Lösung in dein Lernheft.

Teile ihm mit …
1. was man alles einsenden muss
2. die Regeln *(mind. vier)*
3. den Preis
4. wann ein Foto nicht zum Wettbewerb zugelassen wird
5. was geschieht, wenn man mit einem Foto gewonnen hat *(zwei Dinge)*

Unit 1 | Klassenarbeit A

LANGUAGE

___/27

1 WORDS Melanie reports from Australia

___/8

Melanie from Osnabrück is spending a year in Australia living with a family on a farm. Once a week she writes a letter to her class in Germany, in English, of course!

Help Melanie by completing the text with words from the box. Be careful: there are three more words than you need.

> atmosphere • Aussies • barbecue • cancer • careful •
> climate • dirt • emus • gorgeous • instructor • mate •
> outback • ozone • reef • serious • sunscreen •
> ultraviolet • unique • wetsuit

On the farm I met Joey, the 16-year-old son of the family. When I first saw him, I thought he was

_____. I thought that he would be very _____ because

he was showing me my work on the farm, but in fact he spent all his time laughing and making jokes.

To start with I couldn't help laughing with him, but because he was my _____,

I became nervous and began to freak out.

One day he told me about his favourite hobby: he and his _____ like riding their

dirt bikes on _____ roads through the Australian _____.

Sometimes they see animals like _____ and koalas. That's quite impressive, isn't

it? Because the _____ in Australia is so hot and sunny, Joey and his friend have

to put on _____ before they go out even when they're wearing special clothes.

The hole in the _____ layer lets dangerous _____ rays pass

into the atmosphere. Even if you're sitting in the shade, you have to be _____

because the sun is still dangerous. It's a really serious problem and a lot of Australians do develop skin

_____.

After they go for their bike rides, Joey and his mate like to go for a _____ down at

the beach and they invite other friends too. The _____ even have beach parties on

Christmas Day! That must be a really _____ experience!

2 WORDS Tricky translations

___ / 10

*Melanie was surprised when Joey asked her out to an Australian restaurant one evening.
Read what happened and fill in the correct translation of the German words.*

Last Friday was the _____ (groß) day: our date! We met _____ (vor) the farmhouse. I _____ (tragen) my best dress and Joey looked great. He offered to _____ (tragen) my jacket for me – that was very sweet! Joey wanted to _____ (fahren) to the restaurant but the car was broken so we had to wait for another hour and then _____ (fahren) by bus. He _____ (machen) a short call and asked his mate if he could help him repair the car the next day. _____ (während) we were waiting for the bus, we laughed a lot. That was a good start! When we arrived at the restaurant, we took our seats and the waiter _____ (bringen) the menu. It was very difficult to choose because everything sounded great. It _____ (brauchen) us ages to decide and I _____ (brauchen) Joey to help me, but we finally ordered. We talked a lot _____ (während) dinner and Joey was so funny. I have to say that when I first met him, I didn't really like him. He laughed at me because I didn't know how to ride a horse. And then, just three days _____ (vor), I got very angry with him because he was acting like my _____ (groß) brother and correcting me all the time. But _____ (während) our date he was lovely.

It was the chef himself who _____ (bringen) us our dinner! It was fantastic. When the waiter had _____ (bringen) the plates away and we had finished our drinks, we decided to _____ (machen) something else. I thought we should go to the cinema, and Joey agreed. The film was very scary and I was happy that Joey was with me because he's very _____ (groß) so I wasn't afraid in the dark streets after the film. When we got home, he kissed me good night. It was a fantastic date and I hope we'll _____ (machen) it again very soon!

Unit 1 | Klassenarbeit A

3 GRAMMAR Melanie's time in Australia   ___/9

Today is September 1st. Take a look at the pictures to find out what Melanie and Joey did over the past year, what they usually do and what they are doing now in Australia.
*Use either **simple present**, **present progressive**, **simple past** or **past perfect**.*
Write one sentence for each picture using the correct tense.

> **Die Verwendung der Zeiten**
> Sieh dir die Tabelle mit den Signalwörtern an, bevor du die Aufgabe löst. Sie helfen dir dabei, die richtige Zeitform zu wählen. Achte beim Lösen auf die Vorzeitigkeit.
>
> | Tense | Signal Words |
> |---|---|
> | Simple Present | usually, every day, once a week, every year, always, often, never |
> | Present Progressive | now, at the moment |
> | Simple Past | yesterday, last (week, month, year, Friday …) |
> | Past Perfect | before, after |

January 15th

1 / 2

1 / 2

Now

Every day

1 / 2

MEDIATION

____/ 10

Welcome to Queensland!

You are planning a holiday in Australia with your parents. You found the following text on the internet.

Welcome to Queensland!

You like the sun?
You want to enjoy 300 warm and sunny days a year?
Then you should visit Queensland –
where everyone is happy!

Queensland has so much to offer, it will be hard to decide what you'd like to do most.
Outdoor activities are on offer during summer as well as winter, and our fantastic wildlife tours allow you to explore the natural environment of our many animals – a whale watching tour is only one of many possibilities.
If you love adventure, why not go on an adventure tour or visit one of our theme parks?

For lovers of culture, there are galleries, museums and fascinating exhibitions of Aboriginal art and history. Or if you prefer checking out the latest fashions, our shopping centres and markets are Australia's best.

You can experience everyday Australian life and stay in an apartment in the peaceful quiet countryside, or stay in a hotel in a city on the beach. Whatever you choose, you'll never forget your holiday in Queensland!

Your parents don't understand every word so they ask you about the article. Complete the dialogue.

You   Schaut mal, was ich über Queensland im Internet gefunden habe!

Father   Nicht schlecht … Kann man dort Tiere beobachten?

You   _____ (2 Dinge)

Mother Ich bin ja eher für etwas Geschichte …

You   Das ist auch kein Problem. _____

         _____ (2 Dinge)

Father   Gibt es auch etwas Spannenderes?

You   Sicher! _____ (2 Dinge)

Mother Ich würde ja auch gerne ein bisschen einkaufen gehen …

You   Das kannst du auch.

         _____ (2 Dinge)

Father   Wie sieht es denn mit einer Unterkunft aus?

You   _____ (2 Dinge)

Father   Worauf warten wir dann noch? Auf geht's nach Australien!

WRITING

___/20

Feeling homesick

On the plane to Australia, Melanie met Aurélie, a girl from France. Aurélie is also an exchange student and is staying with a family on a farm near Melbourne.
The two girls often write e-mails to each other. In her last e-mail Aurélie was feeling very homesick and lonely. Write Melanie's reply (about 200 words).

You can include …
- Melanie's own experience on the cattle farm,
- her feelings,
- questions about Aurélie's life and feelings,
- some advice.

 E-Mails schreiben

Benutze beim Verfassen deiner E-Mail **linking words** (after some time, suddenly, then, next, but, because, that, who …), **beschreibende Adjektive** (an exciting trip) und **Adverbien** (I missed them terribly).
Achte auf die Verwendung der richtigen Zeiten.
Lies deine E-Mail am Ende noch einmal durch und korrigiere deinen Text.
Weitere Tipps findest du in deinem Englischbuch auf S. 15 und im Skills File auf S. 144–145.

You can start like this:

Dear Aurélie,

I was very sorry to hear that you're not feeling so good at the moment.

SPEAKING

____/16

Bushfire!

As the climate in many parts of Australia is very dry and hot, every year there are many bushfires. These are dangerous for animals and for human beings.

Look at the statistics about bushfires in Australia and explain them. Start by giving a general picture of what the statistics show, then talk in more detail. Finish with a conclusion.

> **Informationen über Statistiken enthalten meist drei Teile:**
> 1. Informationen darüber, was die Statistik zeigt: **The table is about ..., It shows the different ... in/of ... / It compares the size/number of ... with ...**
> 2. Genaue Beschreibungen und Erklärungen: **The chart/table compares the numbers of ..., x has the largest/second-largest/smallest ...**
> 3. Schlussfolgerungen: **So that shows that ..., You can see that ..., To conclude, you can say that ...**
>
> Diese Übung passt zum Skills File auf S. 127 und zur Übung auf S. 10 in deinem Englischbuch. Du kannst die Übung auch schriftlich lösen.

Bushfire statistics – fires on public land in Victoria
Number of fires

Reasons for the fires	Average number of fires each year	Percentage of total[5] fires
Lightning[1]	149	26 %
Deliberate[2]	145	25 %
Agricultural[3]	96	16 %
Campfires	59	10 %
Cigarettes/Matches	41	7 %
Machinery/Exhausts[4]	15	3 %
Cause unknown	37	6 %
Other	42	8 %

Quelle: http://www.dse.vic.gov.au/fire-and-other-emergencies/fire-management/causes-of-bushfire/bushfire-statistics

You can start like this:

> The table shows the different causes of bushfires in Victoria. It compares ...

---

[1] lightning ['laɪtnɪŋ] *Blitzeinschlag* [2] deliberate [dɪ'lɪbərət] *absichtlich, vorsätzlich*
[3] agricultural [ˌægrɪ'kʌltʃərəl] *landwirtschaftlich* [4] exhaust [ɪɡ'zɔːst] *Abgas* [5] total ['təʊtl] *Gesamt-*

Unit 1 — Klassenarbeit B

Gesamtpunktzahl ohne Speaking ____ / 50   Note ____

Gesamtpunktzahl mit Speaking ____ / 65   Note ____

READING ____ / 10

School of the Air Alice Springs

School of the Air Alice Springs – the world's largest classroom

Imagine life in a state where your nearest neighbour lives more than ten kilometres away from you, and the nearest town with a supermarket, cinema and school is a four-hour car-ride. Welcome to Central Australia!

The Alice Springs School of the Air (ASSOA) provides an educational service for about 120 children spread out across million square kilometres of Central Australia. They take part in lessons without having to come to a school building – they are educated by teachers via internet.

These children grow up in a special situation, because their nearest neighbour may live more than ten kilometres from their home. The next family with a child the same age may be as far as 200 km away, and the nearest school might be even further. This is why they need a different form of education.

In many ways the bush children clearly have an advantage over those living in a town or city. They are more active, healthier and freer than many other children. Most learn to ride horses at an early age, and they know how to survive in the outback. Many even know how to brand[1] a horse or cow, to crack a whip or even to drive a car. Others are familiar with Aboriginal traditions or regional plants and animals.

The School of the Air simply adds to this education, and brings in knowledge of the outside world. The students learn how to work independently and organize themselves.

All ASSOA students must have an identified tutor[2], and supervision[3] is required for a minimum of four hours per day.

The lessons at the School of the Air make learning an easier and happier process. This can be seen in the reaction of parents as well as students and their results in class tests. Students can stay at ASSOA until year 9. After that most move away from home to go to boarding school[4].
Years 3, 5 and 7 students are required to participate in the National Assessment Program (NAP)[5] each year. The school is in the top 10% of the education system in the Northern Territory.

[1] (to) brand [brændmɑːk] *brandmarken*   [2] identified tutor [aɪˈdentɪfaɪd tjuːtə] *ausgewiesener Tutor (im Kontakt mit den Lehrern der ASSOA)*   [3] supervision [ˌsuːpəˈrvɪʒn] *Betreuung*   [4] boarding school [ˈbɔːdɪŋ] *Internat*
[5] National Assessment Program: national testing of writing, reading and language skills to judge students' development

a) *Read the text carefully. Tick true, false or not given. (6P)*

		True	False	Not given
1	Children in the outback are less active than city children.			
2	There is no homework at the School of the Air.			
3	Outback children have special skills and know how to survive in the outback.			
4	The School of the Air provides lessons for about 120 students.			
5	Most of them travel a long distance to school every day.			
6	School of the Air students get better grades than students at normal schools.			

b) *Answer the questions with information from the text. (4P)*

1. Why is a School of the Air necessary in some parts of Australia?
2. Describe the communication between teachers and students at the School of the Air.
3. What advantages does the School of the Air offer the students?
4. Look at the text again. What do the students do after year 9?

LANGUAGE

____/ 25

1 WORDS Explaining words

____/ 7

Sometimes you do not know or you forgot how to say things in English. When that happens, you should use other words to describe what you are trying to say. In the following grid a student has started to explain some words. Help him finish his list!

Word	Explanation
independent	
	If you spend time in the sun you will develop this.
	It can be ~ to have a map when you visit a city you've never been to before.
conclusion	
	When you are in bed, you lie on this.
	If your brother thinks that your parents love you more than him, this is how he feels.
poison	

2 GRAMMAR Students at the School of the Air ___ /5

> **Verb + object + *to*-infinitive**
> Nach einigen Verben kann ein Objekt stehen, auf das ein Infinitiv mit **to** folgt.
> Präge dir diese Verben ein:
> (to) ask sb. (not) to do sth.
> (to) force sb. (not) to do sth.
> (to) help sb. to do sth.
> (to) teach sb. (not) to do sth.
> (to) tell sb. (not) to do sth.
> (to) want sb. to do sth.
>
> Achtung! Nach den entsprechenden deutschen Verben steht ein Nebensatz mit „dass".
> Auf die englischen Verben darf jedoch kein that-Satz folgen.

Complete the following interview with a student of the School of the Air.

Interviewer Why do you learn with the School of the Air?

Boy My parents _____

(want – learn with) the School of the Air. There's no school near our house, so they thought it was a good idea for me.

Interviewer Can you describe school life to me and the listeners?

Boy Yes, of course. The computer is in our living room. We communicate via the internet, and the first thing I do in the morning is say hello to my classmates. Sometimes my little sister is still in the room, so I have to _____. (tell – leave)

Then, usually our teacher _____ our homework.

(want – read) Sometimes my father _____

mathematical problems. (help – understand) He _____

harder at school. (want – work) But that's quite difficult when there's nobody around to check if you're doing your school work.

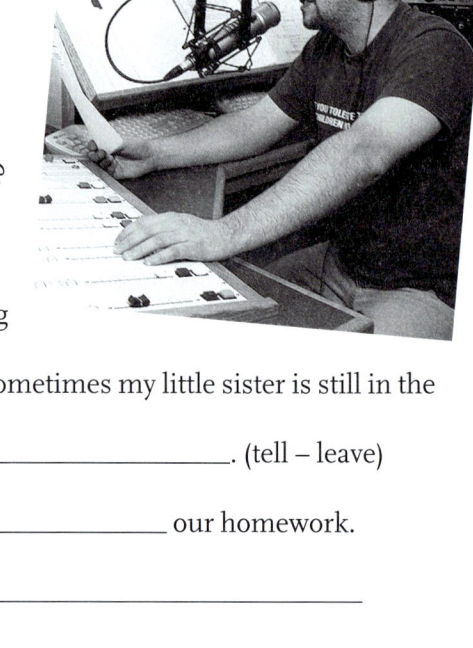

Interviewer So being a student at the School of the Air is not always easy. Let's see what the next student has to say. Thanks for the interview!

Boy No worries!

3 GRAMMAR A new student at the School of the Air

___/5

Robert lives in a town one hundred kilometres away from Alice Springs. He is a new student at the School of the Air, and there are a lot of things he does not know about life at the school. Write down what he does not know or is unsure about using the **to-infinitive**.

I don't know I'm not sure	who where when how what	talk to on the first morning. get my student ID from. do my homework. hand in the assignments. say to my new classmates.

4 GRAMMAR The life of a School of the Air student

___/8

Twice a year a group of experienced students meets new students to welcome them.
They talk about their lives at the School of the Air and answer questions the new students have.
Re-write what they talk about using **infinitives** instead of relative clauses.

1 There is a lot of work which we have to do over the weekend.

_____

_____

2 There are different assignments that we have to complete.

_____

_____

3 We have a teacher who takes care of the new students.

_____

4 During the break I go and see my mum in the kitchen where I can have a cup of tea.

_____

_____

5 I'm happy that there is no uniform which I have to wear.

_____

6 I am the first person in my family who has come to Australia as an exchange student.

_____

_____

7 We had nobody who we could ask for help.

_____

8 At the beginning there are a lot of new things that you have to learn.

_____

_____

WRITING

____/15

Australian Aborigines

*A sad and often unknown part of Australia's history is the story of the Aborigines or Aboriginals.
You have decided to write a report about the Australian Aborigines for your school magazine.*

Use the fact sheet below to write your text.

past:
- 40,000 years ago developed oldest rock art in the world
- 19th century: Aborigines had to move because of European settlers; Aborigines who did not go were killed
- Europeans thought Aborigine culture was primitive
- Number of Aborigines reduced
- 1963: right to vote for Aborigines
- Until 1970s: Aboriginal children taken away from families

today:
- Australia's population: more than 20 million, approx. 2% Aborigines
- Some still don't live in the same place their whole lives, move around within a limited area, some live in tribes
- Oldest members make decisions
- Problems: discrimination, poverty, too much alcohol, unemployment

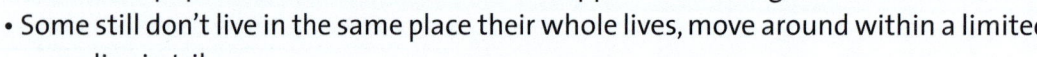

> **Sachtexte schreiben**
> ☐ Verfasse deinen Sachtext nüchtern und ohne Spannung hineinzubringen (zum Beispiel durch ausschmückende Adjektive). Verwende dennoch **linking words** (**but**, **because**, **after** …), um Sätze zu verbinden.
> ☐ Denke an die Verwendung der richtigen Zeit!
> ☐ Verwende keine Kurzformen (**do not** anstatt **don't**).

SPEAKING

____/15

I can tell you more

a) Find yourself a partner and act out the role play together.

Imagine you're staying at a campsite on the east coast of Australia. You meet an Australian boy/girl who is staying in the caravan next to yours.

*Start your conversation very politely and introduce yourselves. Ask and answer questions.
Ask for help if you need to or give help if you are asked. End your conversation in a friendly way.
Take ten minutes to prepare your dialogue.*

> **Sprechen üben**
> ☐ Du und dein Partner könnt euch gegenseitig korrigieren, so funktioniert die Übung am besten.
> ☐ Du kannst den Dialog aber auch jeweils nur für Partner A oder B aufnehmen und mit der Aufnahme jeweils die andere Rolle einsprechen und aufzeichnen. So kannst du dich selbst überprüfen und korrigieren.

Partner A: the German boy/girl	Partner B: the Australian boy/girl

• you arrived the evening before • you're from Frankfurt am Main • you go camping every year • it's your first time at this campsite • you want to find out more about the campsite (pool? / disco? / café? / how far to the beach?) • you're interested in swimming in the sea	• you arrived 10 days ago • you're from Alice Springs, Northern Territory, Australia • you love camping • it's the third time you've been to the campsite, weather always great • you know a lot (pool ▶ near the entrance, café at campsite, opposite supermarket, disco ▶ outside the campsite once a week on Friday ▶ five minutes' walk) • you want to go to the beach in half an hour

b) *Swap roles and imagine you both really hate camping and it's raining cats and dogs. Create a dialogue of the same length as in **a)** with your partner.*

Partner A: the German boy/girl	Partner B: the Australian boy/girl

• you arrived the evening before • you are from Chemnitz • you go camping every year (your first time at this campsite) • you prefer staying in hotels • you want to know which cities your partner likes • you enjoy holidays at the sea because you like swimming and eating fish	• you arrived ten days ago • you are from Cardiff in Wales • this is your third time at the campsite • weather has been bad so far • you hate camping • you like hotels (say why) • you prefer going to different places every year (e.g. Paris, Barcelona, Vienna) • you want to have an ice-cream

Unit 2 — Klassenarbeit A

Gesamtpunktzahl ohne Speaking _____ / 97   Note _____

Gesamtpunktzahl mit Speaking _____ / 110   Note _____

READING _____/5

Different jobs for different people

Read the following job adverts from the Springfield News of February 21st. Then answer the questions.

Retail¹ staff wanted

Work is available in our new department stores and boutiques throughout the country. Most positions are as sales assistants, however there are also stock-taking² jobs. For retail you need fluent English. Experience is helpful but not necessary.

We need help especially in the months leading up to Christmas – particularly in our department stores.

Apply within one of our stores or call Steven at 0207 – 324567 and ask for an appointment for an interview.

Fashcloth Ltd. The Fashion Stores

Call centre agent

If you have sales experience and love to talking to people, this could be the job for you. In most positions you have to make phone calls to sell one of our products. You will need to speak English fluently and be confident about your sales skills. Positions are usually parttime. We offer a great salary (£12 per hour plus bonuses for sales).

Don't hesitate³ to send your application and CV via email to staff@callyou.co.uk.

Callyou Call Centres. Any questions?

Help us harvest

Our apples are one of the most delicious fruits in the world. At Fruitco Bournemouth, we take extra care that their great taste is guaranteed. For the new harvesting season, we need you to help us pick the ripe fruit so that it can be delivered to our valued customers around the world.

However, it is hard physical work and – even in England – sometimes in hot weather.
As we pay you by the amount you pick, you'll earn more as you become more experienced.

Send an application to *Fruitco*, 893A Castle Lane West, Bournemouth, Dorset BH8 9UA.

1   Where will you earn more money the more successful you are?

2   Which job do you need to have experience for?

3   What kind of jobs is the department store offering?

4   What do you have to be prepared for when you work as an apple picker?

5   What qualifications do you need to have when you work in a call centre?

¹ retail [riːteɪl] *Einzelhandel*   ² stock-taking [stɒkteɪkɪŋ] *Inventur*   ³ (to) hesitate [ˈhezɪteɪt] *zögern*

WRITING

____/20

Applying for a job

Choose **a)** or **b)**.

a) Apply for one of the jobs described in the adverts in the reading exercise. Write an application letter. Write something about your skills and why you would be the right person for this job.

b) Sue Evans lives in Bristol. She has seen the advert below and wants to apply for the job. Write her application letter. Write something about her skills and why she would be the right person for this job.

> **Förmliche Briefe** *(formal letters)*
> - Adresse ohne Namen
> - vollständige Anschrift
> - Datum
> - höfliche Anrede
> - Langformen verwenden
> - Brief in Absätze gliedern
> - Ende: Dank im Voraus, höfliche Schlussformel, Unterschrift, getippter Name
>
> Einen Beispielbrief findest du im Skills File auf S. 146 in deinem Englischbuch.

The Bristol Times 2 November 2011

St. John's Residential Care Home[1]

At St. John's we have 80 residents[2] and consider it extremely important to offer each one of them a wide range of free-time activities.

We are looking for a **young volunteer** (m/f) to teach a small group (12 people) basic computer skills, including using the internet and writing e-mails.

The classes would take place once a week for one hour. If you know how to use the internet effectively and know a bit about downloading programs and how to surf the internet safely, you are the right person for this job! And don't be afraid – you don't have to be an internet expert to apply, but you should be able to explain things so that your "students" find their way round the internet.

Are you interested in working with people and sharing your IT skills?
We would provide training after Christmas.
Please tell us which days of the week would suit you best.

Sorry, we can't pay anything, but we will be happy to give you a reference.
Please send your application letter plus CV to:

Ms Alice Spring
St. John's Residential Care Home
4 New Garden Street, Bristol BS1 3AD

---

[1] Residential Care Home [ˌrezɪˈdenʃl keə(r) həʊm] *Pflegeheim*   [2] resident [ˈrezɪdənt] *Bewohner/in, Anwohner/in*

LANGUAGE

___/51

1 WORDS Jobs

___/21

a) Make a mind map for the topic "jobs". Use the new vocabulary from Unit 2. The numbers tell you how many words you should be able to add to each word group. You can add more words as you work through the unit. (17P)

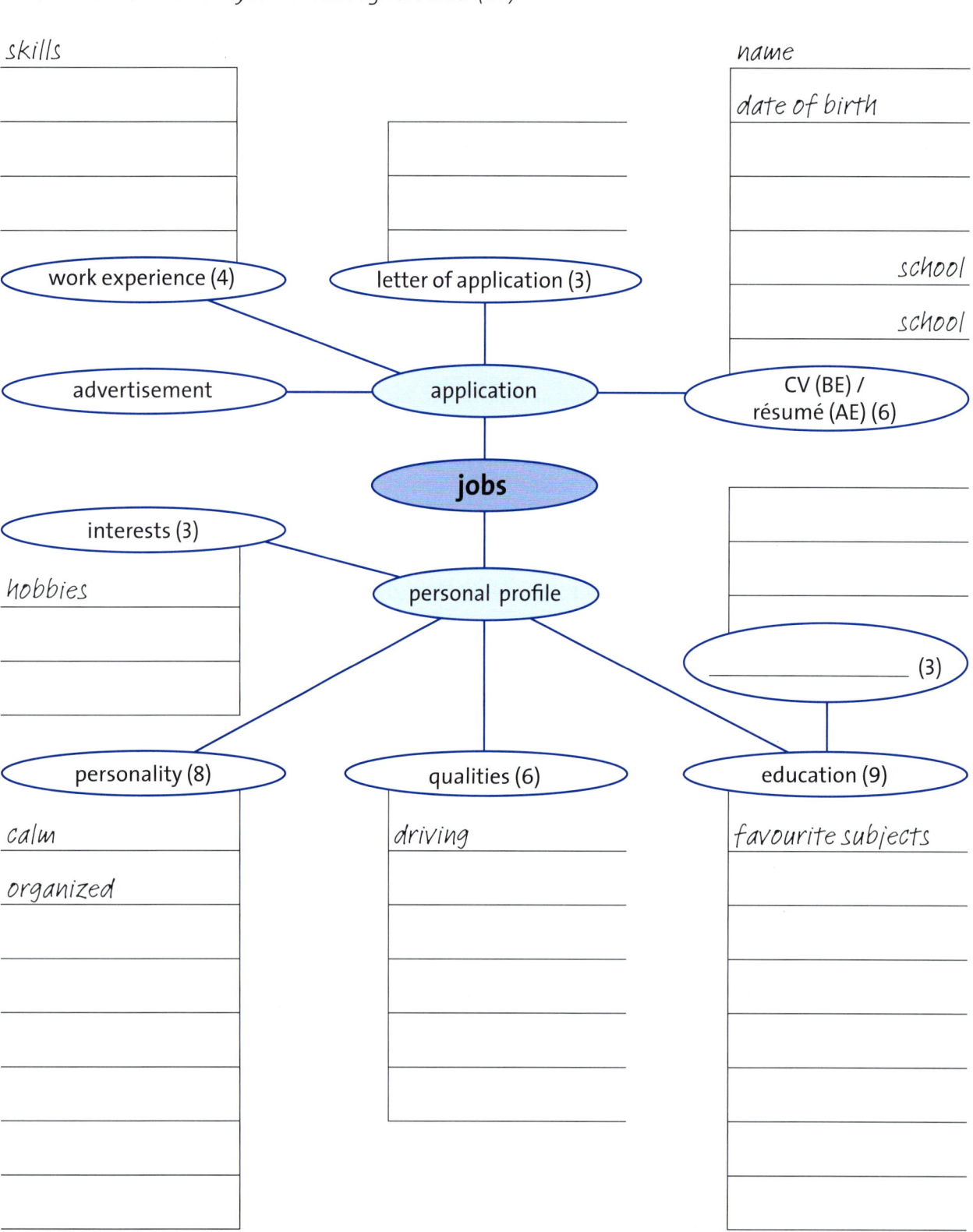

b) Choose **four** words from your mind map and write sentences for each one in your exercise book. (4P)

2 WORDS Nigel's nightmare of getting a job   ____ / 5

Nigel has written twenty applications for almost every job advert he could find, but so far he has only received letters of rejection¹.

Re-write his thoughts using **negative prefixes**.

1 Sometimes I have the feeling that it is *not possible* to get the perfect job.

_____

2 So far I have*n't* been *lucky* in finding a job.

_____

3 I did*n't* feel very *comfortable* at my last interview.

_____

4 It would*n't* be *polite* to tell the manager that you think his tie looks awful.

_____

5 You take a big risk² if you apply for a job and your CV is*n't accurate*.

_____

3 GRAMMAR This is me!   ____ / 10

Complete Timmy's description by using the words in the box below. Use **gerunds**.

| do (2x) • eat • get • go • hang • lead • listen to • play • ride |

My name is Timmy and I am good at _____ football and _____ other people's problems. At least this is what people say. I like _____ to the cinema with my best friend Tony. _____ around with friends from school is great fun! _____ a healthy life is also important for me. I stay fit by _____ lots of sports and _____ all my vegetables. I am keen on _____ my scooter. I'm always very serious about environmental issues³ without _____ involved in politics. After I leave school, I want to study law and become a judge. Well, what else ...? Ah, yes. What I don't like is _____ homework. It ruins my whole day, I can tell you.

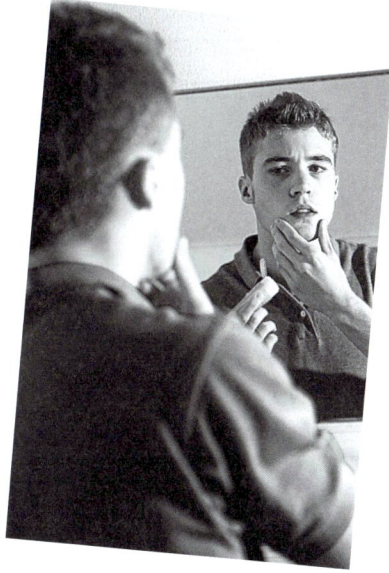

¹ rejection [rɪˈdʒekʃn] *Absage, Ablehnung*   ² risk [rɪsk] *Risiko*   ³ issue [ˈɪʃuː] *Thema, Problem*

4 WORDS Translating „Möglichkeit"

In German, all of the following sentences contain the word „Möglichkeiten". Choose the correct English expression.

1. Have you had the _____ to contact the job agency yet?

2. There are a number of _____ to apply for a job.

3. Have you thought of the _____ of asking for a job in the shop?

4. The _____ of getting a job without an interview are very small indeed.

5. There is no _____ of getting to this place without a car.

6. We have the _____ of going to Madame Tussaud's when we are in London.

5 GRAMMAR Things the employer tells you

____/9

*The manager of the company at which you applied for a job tells you a lot about working there. Write what he says. Use **gerunds**.*

1. not wear – helmet – dangerous
2. should not mind – get your hands dirty
3. this job – good – if you like – get to know – new people
4. ask – other workers – helpful
5. take – too many toilet breaks – not appreciated
6. make – personal phone calls – can get you into trouble
7. be late – for work – can also cause problems
8. avoid – have – too long lunch breaks
9. fancy – work abroad?
10. can imagine – send you to our Australian branch

1. *Not wearing a helmet is dangerous.*
2. _____
3. _____
4. _____
5. _____
6. _____
7. _____
8. _____
9. _____
10. _____

☞ Mehr Übungen zu **gerunds** und **infinitives** findest du in Klassenarbeit B.

STUDY SKILLS

___/21

Getting a scholarship[1] for the USA

Imagine you want to spend a year in the USA but you haven't got enough money to do that.

Fortunately, there are organizations which support young students who wish to study abroad by offering them a scholarship. To apply for this, you need to send in a formal application letter as well as your CV, which should give an insight into your activities at school and your extracurricular activities. Write your CV.

> **Einen Lebenslauf schreiben**
> - Name, Adresse, Telefonnummer, E-Mail-Adresse
> - Personal statement, in dem du dich kurz beschreibst
> - Lückenlose Darstellung deiner schulischen Laufbahn und erworbener Abschlüsse
> - Auflistung deiner beruflichen Laufbahn, z. B. Praktika, Ferienjobs
> - Deine Fähigkeiten, Hobbys, Interessen
> - Kurse oder Preise
> - Angabe außerschulischer Aktivitäten und Qualifikationen, z. B. Schülersprecher, Trainer
>
> Der Lebenslauf wird nicht unterschrieben. Ein Bild gehört zwar nicht unbedingt dazu, wird aber oft im Rahmen der Bewerbungsunterlagen gefordert.
> Ein Beispiel für einen Lebenslauf findest du auf S. 38 in deinem Englischbuch, Tipps auf S. 148.

[1] scholarship ['skɒləʃɪp] *Stipendium*

Unit 2 | Klassenarbeit A

SPEAKING

____/13

🎧 03 **An assessment centre – Part 1**

*Think of a job you would like to apply for. Imagine you sent an application and a CV to the company.
A few days later you received a message on your answerphone. The manager of the company called you and suggested two possible dates. Listen to what he says.*

🎧 04 **Now you**

*Call the company to confirm the date and ask for further information.
Press "pause" when you hear the beep. Press "play" when you've said your part.*

1 *The manager of Boxcom and partners*
▼

You Sage wer du bist, bedanke dich für die Nachricht und frage nach, ob es sich um ein Assessment Center oder ein Vorstellungsgespräch handelt. (3P)

2 *Manager*
▼

You Sage, dass du nicht genau weißt, was ein Assessment Center ist und frage nach einer Erläuterung. (2P)

3 *Manager*
▼

You Frage, ob du es richtig verstanden hast, dass die erfolgreiche Teilnahme am Assessment Center die Voraussetzung für eine Einladung zu einem Vorstellungsgespräch ist. (2P)

4 *Manager*
▼

You Bestätige den Termin und frage nach der genauen Adresse. (2P)

5 *Manager*
▼

You Sage, dass das unproblematisch ist. Du kennst den Weg dorthin. Du hast keine weiteren Fragen. (3P)

6 *Manager*
▼

You Bedanke dich. (1P)

7 *Manager*
▼

Klassenarbeit B

Unit 2

27

Gesamtpunktzahl ohne Speaking _____/59 Note _____

Gesamtpunktzahl mit Speaking _____/73 Note _____

LISTENING

_____/22

🎧 05 **Are you happy with your job?**

The radio programme Radio Today has a themed week on the topic "Are you happy with your job".
Each morning between 10 and 11 another person is interviewed.

a) *Read the sentences carefully. Then listen to Terry and Alice.*
Are the statements true or false? Correct the wrong sentences. (11P)

		True	False	Why
1	Alice hasn't always been happy with her job, but her career is going well now.	☐	☐	
2	Alice doesn't like her job because she doesn't have much free time anymore.	☐	☐	
3	Alice knew from the start what she wanted to do after school.	☐	☐	
4	After school Alice started to work at her father's computer shop.	☐	☐	
5	Alice worked in a supermarket and thought about her interests.	☐	☐	
6	Alice has a boutique with one of her friends now.	☐	☐	
7	Alice has made her hobby her job.	☐	☐	

Unit 2 | Klassenarbeit B

06 b) *Listen to Terry and Harry. Then tick a), b), c) or d). (5P)*

1	After finishing school Harry ...	a) did secretarial jobs.	☐
		b) did some work experience.	☐
		c) worked in a supermarket.	☐
		d) spent a year abroad.	☐
2	Harry became a careers advisor because ...	a) this was his dream job.	☐
		b) he got the chance to do some special training.	☐
		c) he didn't know what else to do.	☐
		d) he had had many problems in finding the perfect job himself.	☐
3	Harry works only part-time as a careers advisor because ...	a) he decided to find out about his strengths.	☐
		b) he doesn't need the money.	☐
		c) he decided to focus on his book.	☐
		d) he has to travel a lot to give interviews about his book.	☐
4	Harry likes his job very much because ...	a) he can work at home.	☐
		b) he gives other people advice and makes them happy.	☐
		c) he gets to know a lot of people.	☐
		d) he gets nice presents from the readers of his book.	☐
5	Harry wrote the book because ...	a) he wanted to help young people through the jungle of job applications.	☐
		b) he wanted to become a successful author.	☐
		c) he found his job boring and wanted to try something different.	☐
		d) he wanted to give young people advice about job interviews.	☐

c) *Listen to Harry's tips and complete the table.*
Write down three tips each about what applicants should do and should not do. (6P)

Shoulds	Should nots
_____	_____
_____	_____
_____	_____
_____	_____

LANGUAGE   ____/25

1 WORDS The downside of being rich   ____/9

Michael H. (17) has made a fortune by creating webpages for big companies. Here he tells you why being rich is not always a blessing.

Read his text and fill in the correct word from the box in the correct form.

> (to) advise • ambition • calm • confident • design • determination •
> (to) determine • employee • faith in • (to) focus • fortune • greedy •
> (to) impress • necessary • responsible • stressful • university • within

It all started because I wanted to _____ my classmates at school. I have always been interested in computers and games, so I decided to _____ on creating websites for companies. At my uncle's birthday party I met a guy who was successful in that kind of work, and he _____ me to concentrate on special _____ which nobody had ever done before. I was _____ to start my own business and so I decided not to go to _____. I told my parents that it wasn't _____ for me to study and to my great surprise they stayed _____. The more pages I created, the more my _____ grew and my _____ to achieve more. I was _____ for my own projects! My little business became very successful and I soon needed _____. My _____ myself increased and I became more _____. I thought I could make my _____ in this business. However, _____ a few months I lost something which I had never enjoyed as much as I could: I realized I wasn't a child anymore. I was leading the _____ life of a _____ adult!

Unit 2 | Klassenarbeit B

2 GRAMMAR Stop being lazy and get a job   ___/9

Nigel was eventually successful with one of his applications and he got invited to a job interview.
He is so excited about it! Read his thoughts and use the correct form of the verbs to make correct sentences.

> ☞ Nach den Verben **to forget**, **to remember**, **to stop** und **to try** kann sowohl ein Gerundium als auch ein **to**-Infinitiv stehen. Beachte dabei die unterschiedlichen Bedeutungen.

I _____ (remember, talk) to my teacher about applications last year.

He told me to _____ (stop, make) so many mistakes in my

application letters. I tried really hard, but he still always found a lot of mistakes in the applications I

showed him. I'll never _____ (forget, listen) to all the feedback he

gave me. For practice, I _____ (tried, write) as many applications as

I could. And I even _____ (stop, play) football with my friends or

_____ (go) to the cinema with them after school. I also improved my CV. One day I sent an

application to a company. I was very nervous and in the meantime I even _____

(try, do) yoga to calm myself down. One week later I got a letter and now I have a job interview, I'm so

happy! I mustn't _____ (forget, call) my mother after the interview

and I must _____ (remember, say) thank you to my teacher.

3 GRAMMAR We want you!   ___/7

Read this notice from a school's notice board. Take one preposition and one verb from the box and complete the text. Be careful: there is one more preposition and one more verb than you need.

> ☞ Nach einer **Präposition (by, for, of, without, ...)** folgt das Verb als **Gerundium**.

about • at • in (2x) • of (2x)
• on • to
be • earn • explain • help •
spend • talk • teach • write

Are you interested _____ some extra money?

Are you used _____ your favourite subject to other students?

Are you interested _____ exercises?

Are you good _____ ideas and concepts?

Are you keen _____ younger students from your school?

Are you tired _____ afternoons alone?

Do you dream _____ a teacher?

Then join our school's homework club and help younger students in your favourite subject!
For further information ask Mr Lee.

MEDIATION

____/12

A job for your exchange partner

Your exchange partner Pete from England is staying with you for the summer holidays. He has found an advert for a summer job but doesn't understand everything, so he asks you to explain some things to him.

Read the advert, then answer your partner's questions in English on page 32.

Aushilfe in der Touristeninformation gesucht!

Jedes Jahr kommen Tausende Besucher aus allen Ländern der Erde nach Stuttgart. Hier finden sie Erholung, attraktive Freizeitangebote und ein breites Spektrum an Einkaufsmöglichkeiten. Nicht zuletzt sind auch unsere hervorragenden Restaurants ein beliebtes Ziel für Liebhaber saisonaler Küche.

Für die Zeit der Sommerferien suchen wir deshalb eine englischsprachige Aushilfe in unserer Touristeninformation für unsere Gäste aus den USA. Sie müssen nicht unbedingt über Erfahrungen im Tourismus verfügen und auch keine Kenntnisse über unsere Stadt mitbringen.

Ihre Aufgaben werden sein, Touristen am Flughafen zu begrüßen und ihnen ein Informationsblatt auszuhändigen. In der Touristeninformation werden Sie dann alle englischen Fragen an unsere ausgebildeten Mitarbeiter weitergeben. Ihre Arbeitszeit ist montags bis samstags von 9.00 bis 18:30 Uhr.

Wir erwarten von Ihnen ein sicheres Auftreten sowie hervorragende Englischkenntnisse. Pünktlichkeit und Zuverlässigkeit sind darüber hinaus selbstverständlich.

Wir bieten Ihnen einen überdurchschnittlichen Verdienst von € 12,00 pro Stunde.

Interesse? Dann schauen Sie doch einfach direkt in der Touristeninformation am Marktplatz vorbei und fragen Sie dort nach Frau Eigel.

Tourismusverband Stuttgart
0711 – 34 56 78.

Unit 2 | Klassenarbeit B

Pete Well, this is the advert I found in the newspaper. What kind of job is it exactly?

You _____

_____

Pete And what do I have to do? *(three things)*

You _____

_____

Pete That sounds good to me. But don't I have to know the area for this job?

You _____

_____

Pete But what skills do I need? *(three things)*

You _____

_____

Pete When do I have to work?

You _____

_____

Pete But I'm only here for the summer holidays.

You _____

_____

Pete OK then. How can I apply for it? *(two things)*

You _____

_____

SPEAKING

____/14

An assessment centre – Part 2

Now you arrive at the Boxcom assessment centre. The first task is to give a presentation for five minutes about yourself, your skills and why you applied for this job.

Make notes for your speech and practise it. If possible, record it and check your results.

> **Sprechen üben**
> Auch beim Sprechen solltest du dich kontrollieren. Du kannst deinen Vortrag aufnehmen oder eine andere Person bitten, deinen Vortrag anzuhören und dir später eine Rückmeldung zu geben.
> Achte auf:
> - Gliederung des Vortrags,
> - korrekte Zeitformen,
> - flüssiges Sprechen.

You can use the following table for your preparation.

Personal information	Name:
	Age:
	City in which you live:
Education	
What your interests are (should have something to do with the job)	
What your skills are (should have something to do with the job)	
Why you applied for the job	
What makes you the best person for the job	

Unit 3 — Klassenarbeit A

Gesamtpunktzahl ohne Speaking _____ / 72   Note _____

Gesamtpunktzahl mit Speaking _____ / 82   Note _____

LISTENING   _____ / 10

🎧 07 **Women's Rights Are Human Rights**

Listen to this famous speech which was originally given by the former First Lady of the USA, Hillary Rodham Clinton, in Beijing in China on September 5th, 1995.

a) Complete the sentences. (5P)

1 Women come together _____.

2 When women come together _____.

3 However different women may appear, _____
_____.

4 Let us create a world _____.

5 Every family _____.

b) Are the following statements right or wrong? Correct the wrong sentences. (5P)

Clinton says …

1 Women are educated all over the world.
_____
_____

2 Women share a common future.
_____
_____

3 A world should be created where all women treat men with respect.
_____
_____

4 If women are treated equally, this leads to healthy families, and healthy families lead to healthy communities.
_____
_____

5 Women's lives can't get better.
_____
_____

LANGUAGE ____/ 32

1 WORDS Forms of government ____/6

Complete the following table with words that belong to different forms of government.

Form of government	Who has the power?
absolute monarchy	
	the rich
	one single person
anarchy	
	the citizens
	religious leaders

2 WORDS Talking about politics ____/7

Can you find the right words? Complete the sentences.

1 If you support somebody with all your heart and want her/him to succeed, you _____ her/him.

2 Germany is a _____ state, because the citizens have the right to vote for their government.

3 Many countries have _____ problems, as they are suffering from the consequences of the financial crisis.

4 Our neighbour is on the city _____.

5 People _____ the mayor of their city.

6 For four years he _____ over meetings.

7 Since they want to win the election, political _____ often promise the earth, but have to change their position afterwards when they are faced with reality.

3 WORDS What was that again? ____/5

Here are some more new words from Unit 3. Explain them in your own words.

1 assembly: _____

2 screenplay: _____

3 xenophobic: _____

4 agenda: _____

5 to oppose sb./sth.: _____

4 GRAMMAR Poor people and human rights

____/5

Jason has to hold a short talk about poor people and their rights for his English class.

Here are some key words which he noted down. Make complete sentences using **present participles**.

1. Although – everybody should have – same rights – tourists watch – a lot of poor people – hang around – in the streets
2. They notice – the rights of – people live in slums – are limited
3. In townships – they see – children – play – in front of houses which are falling down – whereas – their own children have – right to education
4. If they see – man – steal a woman's handbag – they not realize – he fight – for his right – live
5. It great – listen to – people – play traditional music – and use – their right – express themselves

> **The present participle after certain verbs**
> Nach Verben der Wahrnehmung, z. B. **feel**, **hear**, **listen to**, **notice**, **see**, **smell**, **watch**, folgt ein Objekt sowie das Partizip Präsens: I **heard** the baby **crying** next door.
> Weitere Beispiele findest du im Grammar File 10.3 auf S. 176 in deinem Englischbuch.

1 _____

2 _____

3 _____

4 _____

5 _____

5 GRAMMAR Human rights are for everybody

____/4

Ranjid lives in India. He is writing an essay about human rights.

*Shorten the sentences using **present** or **past participle clauses**.*

Gebrauch von Partizipialsätzen
- Partizipialsätze können **Nebensätze der Zeit oder des Grundes** verkürzen. Sie werden in Gesprächen allerdings weniger häufig verwendet.
- Partizipialsätze können Zusatzinformationen geben und zeitgleiche Vorgänge beschreiben.
- Weitere Beispiele findest du im Grammar File 10.4 und 10.5 auf S. 177–178 in deinem Englischbuch.

As they believe in different things, people should have the freedom of religion.

_____

They should be able to choose their politicians and tell them what they really want for their country.

_____

_____

Many people around the world demonstrate for human rights and are accompanied by a large number of celebrities.

_____

_____

When people enjoy freedom of speech, they can work to improve their country.

_____

_____

6 GRAMMAR Young people and their rights

____ /5

Ranjid asks his friend Peter about the rights young people have in Germany.
Peter sends him an e-mail.
*Shorten his sentences by using **participle clauses**.*
*You will need the conjunctions **after, before, when** and **while**.*

1 You can't work more than two hours a day while you are still going to school.

    _____

    _____

2 Children under the age of 16 must be accompanied by an adult when they visit a pub.

    _____

    _____

3 You are allowed to leave school after you have completed 12 years.

    _____

    _____

4 You have to wait until you are 16 and a half before you learn to drive.

    _____

    _____

5 Before you reach the age of 16 you need your parents' permission to get married.

    _____

    _____

WRITING

____ / 30

Landslide hits an orphanage

Read this article, taken from a newspaper. Then do tasks **a)** and **b)** on p. 40.

Landslide[1] hits orphanage[2] – six children dead

Six children lost their lives today when a landslide hit an orphanage in a peaceful village near Mumbai. "I heard a loud noise and suddenly I was covered in earth and dust. I had to run for my life," said eye-witness Terki Suleiman.

Hundreds of rescue workers tried their best to find survivors, but after five hours searching they had only found dead bodies.

"I was the one who found the first child," said Andy McDowell, a volunteer with the Red Cross in India. "I couldn't stop crying. I just can't believe what happened here."

Not all the bodies have been found yet, but six children aged eight to ten are believed to have lost their lives in the landslide. The boy found by McDowell was taken to hospital immediately, but he could not be saved. "It was too late for him," Martin Andrews, a doctor at the Red Cross Hospital Mumbai, explained. "When I examined him, I couldn't do anything more for him."

The landslide is a disaster for the orphanage, which is in a poor region of India. Three adults, who were working at the orphanage, are also reported missing.

Local charities and this newspaper had warned officials that the orphanage buildings were not safe and that there might be a catastrophe. But they were not listened to! Now it is the children who have to pay the price!

It was still raining when our reporter arrived at the scene. "This terrible rain is preventing us from trying to rescue the missing boys and girls," McDowell told us. More than 100 officials, firefighters and volunteers from the Red Cross stood in a circle unable to believe what had happened. "The children were having their dinner when the mud fell over them," said Geraldine Guetta, manager of the orphanage, wiping away her tears. "The roof couldn't carry the heavy load and collapsed, burying the children underneath it. They didn't have time to escape."

Nearby buildings have been evacuated as officials fear another landslide tonight.

---

[1] landslide ['lændslaɪd] *Erdrutsch* [2] orphanage ['ɔːfənɪdʒ] *Waisenhaus*

a) Write a **summary** of the article in your exercise book. (15P)

 Summary writing
1. **Markiere** alle **wichtigen Fakten**, die dir Antworten auf die **Wh-Fragen** geben (**Who? What? Where? When? Why?**) und halte sie in **Stichpunkten** fest.
2. **Klammere unwichtige Details**, Adjektive, rhetorische Fragen, wörtliche Rede und persönliche Kommentare **ein**. Diese gehören nicht in die Summary.
3. Stelle dir vor, du müsstest **jemandem, der den Text nicht gelesen hat**, erklären, worum es darin geht: Fasse den Text **in eigenen Worten** zusammen und verwende **simple present**. Weitere Hilfen findest du im Skills File auf S. 149 in deinem Englischbuch.

b) Write a **report** for your school magazine about the accident. Inform your fellow students and give the most important facts. (15P)

 Writing a report
1. Finde eine Überschrift.
2. Erwähne in einem einleitenden, **zusammenfassenden Satz**, was passiert ist.
3. Nenne erst die wichtigen Informationen und anschließend die Details. Dabei kannst du dich an den **Wh-Fragen** (**Who? What? Where? When? Why?**) orientieren.
4. Schreibe deinen Bericht im **simple past**, ohne reißerische Adjektive oder direkte Rede. Es geht lediglich um eine **nüchterne und sachliche Darstellung von Fakten**. Schildere das Geschehen, ohne es zu kommentieren.

SPEAKING

____/10

🎧 08 **Slumdog Millionaire (Giving an oral summary)**

Pat and his father Tom are having breakfast. Tom reads out an article he found in The Guardian to his son. Listen to Tom.

*Give an **oral summary** of the article Tom read out. You can record your summary and play it to your parents or teacher to check how you have done.*

 Oral summary
- Wenn du etwas, das du gehört, gesehen oder gelesen hast, **mündlich** zusammenfasst, tust du dies oft **spontan**. Du kannst also nicht lang überlegen und solltest auch nicht zu lang reden.
- Gib nur **das Wesentliche** in eigenen Worten wieder, so wie bei einer schriftlichen **Summary**.
- Halte dich mit deiner eigenen Meinung zurück.
- Denke auch an die **Betonung** dir wichtiger Schlüsselbegriffe oder Themen.
- Verwende **simple present**.

Klassenarbeit B

Unit 3

Gesamtpunktzahl _____ / 79   Note _____

READING

_____ / 33

Read this article taken from the educational section of an American newspaper. Then complete the tasks on page 42.

School students act against school rules

For many teachers the situation in their classrooms and at their schools has become more and more difficult in recent years. "My students tend to lose interest in school subjects early on," says Ann Smith, a math teacher at Highland College in Boston. "Students are becoming more and more aggressive, they break school rules und bully each other, no matter how strict the school rules are. This has a negative effect on our school life and lessons, and it is getting worse. The victims of the bullies, on the other hand, often don't dare to say anything. They don't use their right to get a good education."

School teachers address parents for help

Mike Liberty, teacher for P.E. and math at a small town college 50 miles west of Boston, has noticed the same problems. "Many of our students are more interested in going shopping or playing video games than in learning about politics, for example. They seem to be frustrated, but don't take the opportunity to get involved and improve their situation." He understands that it is hard to look optimistically into the future in these hard times, but during the past few years, he has noticed that young people seem to be less willing to try and change anything. In his opinion, it is the students' responsibility to start to work against problems at school and act democratically.

"Not only children but also parents are often part of the problem. Parents don't show their children that it is important to take part in school life," says Anne Perfew, an educational advisor, working with schools in Massachusetts. "These days, it has become more important than ever for parents, as 'education consumers', to know about the school's ideas and concepts but also about their rights and responsibilities," says principal Mike Tannors. Parents cannot only rely on the school's newsletter or occasional conversations with one or two of the teachers or 'education distributors', they should act as a role model for their children and participate in school affairs. As he puts it, quite often parents seem to know their car mechanic better than their kids' teachers. "If children were cars, their owners would be a lot better informed about their options – they would check on safety features, new innovations and simply the best buy for their money."

Children have a very brief time during which to learn the most important rules and values so they know how to behave correctly in public and get their educational basics right. "It is necessary that parents assist by keeping this small window of opportunity open. By helping their children behave better, they help them learn better too," Perfew states.

A solution to this problem can only be found when schools and parents work together. Lynne Smith, head teacher of Maryland College, is already working against these harmful trends. "Four times a year, we run a school's parliament debate with teachers, parents and students about school life. We talk about problems which exist and how to solve them. We encourage our students to express their opinions. The beginning was a bit difficult, but it has become more and more popular. We are now even seeing a trend towards organizing committees outside the school walls, fighting for young people's rights on a local basis. This is a great success and has improved our everyday life very much."

Unit 3 | Klassenarbeit B

a) *Complete the sentences in your own words. (9P)*

1 In the text, teachers are described as 'education distributors', so parents can be seen as _____ .

2 More and more students are aggressive. They _____ _____ .

3 Instead they _____ _____ .

4 In many families, the parents _____ _____ .

5 It is very important that parents know _____ and _____ .

6 If children were cars, parents _____ .

7 Their relationship to the car mechanic _____ _____ .

8 It would be much easier if _____ .

9 In Maryland, this has been achieved by _____ _____ .

b) *Write a summary of the article. (13P)*

☞ Tipps zum **Summary writing** findest du auf S. 40.

c) *Should parents be more involved in their children's school life?* **Comment** *in about* **100** *words. (11P)*

> ☞ **Einen Kurzkommentar schreiben**
> In einem Kurzkommentar beziehst du Stellung zu einem Zitat oder einer (manchmal provokanten) These. Es geht nicht darum, zu erraten, was deine Lehrerin oder dein Lehrer gern hören möchte – **deine eigene Meinung** ist gefragt!
> - Überlege dir eine **These** und stütze diese mit einem **Argument**.
> - Nenne ein **Gegenargument** und versuche dieses mit deinen Argumenten zu entkräften: **On the one hand …, on the other hand …**
> - Schreibe auch zu kurzen Texten eine **Einleitung** und einen zusammenfassenden **Schlusssatz**.

Unit 3 | Klassenarbeit B   43

LANGUAGE

____ / 31

1 WORDS A crossword

____ / 13

Complete the crossword with the correct words.

Across

3   To hurt someone or yourself

5   People from different countries living together in a new city or country; a name for a place

6   A stronger word for fairness, relating to the law

7   Nobody was hurt or arrested at the demonstration, it was a … protest.

8   When people have the same rights (noun)

10 To be against something

12 Many old people have gained a lot of this.

13 Untidy

Down

1   To give the main ideas of a text

2   Politicians work on this before they discuss it in parliament.

4   All you have learned or read about something.

9   A conference or meeting needs this so that participants know what is going to happen.

11 To destroy something

2 WORDS Prepositions ___/10

*Delia has to write a text about the history of Great Britain, but she is not sure about the prepositions. Complete her text with the correct **prepositions**.*

1 Years ago the people who lived _____ Britain were called Celts.

2 Later, most _____ Britain became a colony _____ the Roman Empire.

3 _____ 1066, the Normans defeated the Anglo-Saxons.

4 The Puritans couldn't practise their religion freely _____ they sailed to America.

5 When Britain won the war against France, they gained control _____ Canada and India.

6 Many people had prejudices _____ black people.

7 The movement _____ Indian independence grew _____ the Second World War.

8 _____ proud supporters of the monarchy, Ruth and her friends watched William and Kate's wedding from start to finish.

3 GRAMMAR Be active for human rights! ___/8

Josh wants to write a leaflet for a human rights organization.
*Change the sentences he has written into the **passive** voice.*

1 In our organization we defend human rights.
   _____

2 We are preparing a charity event for Africa at the moment.
   _____

3 Last year our organization published reports about Africa.
   _____

4 Next month we will publish a report on human rights in South America.
   _____

5 We have also told our members about the lives of poor people.
   _____

6 Political leaders have not given them the same rights.
   _____

7 Cruel landlords made many of them homeless.
   _____

8 We still have to prepare different concepts for our next meeting.
   _____

MEDIATION

____ / 15

What young people in Britain are allowed to do

*You have to write an **essay** about the drinking law in the UK for school. In your research, you have found this text on the web.*

*Write the **essay** in German.*

> **Mediation heißt nicht Übersetzen!**
> Bei dieser Aufgabe kommt es nicht darauf an, wortwörtlich ins Deutsche zu übersetzen. Die Aufgabe besteht im genauen Lesen und sinngemäßen Übertragen des Wesentlichen ins Deutsche.

In the UK, children under five must not be given any alcohol unless supervised or ordered by a doctor in an emergency.

If you want to buy alcohol, you have to be at least 18 years old. If you are between 16 and 17, you may consume wine, beer or cider on licensed premises, but only if you have a meal there too. In England and Wales, these drinks must be ordered by an adult. In Scotland, you do not have to be accompanied when you order alcohol at a restaurant and you are older than 16.

In order to be allowed to buy alcohol in the supermarket, you have to be 18. If you want to buy chocolates filled with spirits or liqueur, you need to be 16 years old. This, however, is very rarely checked by the cashiers.

You need to be aware that you might be asked for ID if you look younger than 21 and want to buy alcohol. In many shops and supermarkets, you will find a sign that informs you of this. If you fail to show any ID, you won't be allowed to buy alcohol, even if you are in fact older than 18.

Supermarkets and shops which are found to be selling alcohol to minors can lose their licence to sell alcohol.

Unit 4 — Klassenarbeit A

Gesamtpunktzahl ohne Speaking _____ / 103   Note _____

Gesamtpunktzahl mit Speaking _____ / 120   Note _____

LISTENING

_____ / 36

🎧 09 **How social is the social network?**

Mr Fitzgerald, a teacher, is looking for a book in the school library. He meets his students Brian and Sarah. Listen to their discussion. Then work on the tasks.

1 Who said what?

_____ / 20

a) *Write the numbers of the statements under the photos. Be careful: there are three more statements than you need.* (10P)

Mr Fitzgerald

Sarah

Brian

_____   _____   _____

1   Does Facebook have anything to do with faces?

2   It's where people meet other people.

3   Facebook was invented at Harvard University.

4   Obviously it's easy to communicate with people all over the world.

5   I'm keeping in touch with friends I can't see every day.

6   There are certain employers who browse through social networking sites to find out information about the people who work for them.

7   Parents or teachers should surf the net together with children.

8   Young people should be made aware of the dangers linked to social networking sites.

9   If you're careful with your profile, only your friends can access your information and your photos.

10   Spam e-mails are a big problem with the internet.

11   I'm very proud of having 150 Facebook friends.

12   I hope that I will find a boyfriend there.

13   I only use the internet from time to time.

b) *Answer the questions using **key words** or **numbers**. You do not need to write complete sentences.* (10P)

1. What are Brian and Sarah doing in the library?

2. Why does Brian not want Sarah to check her Facebook page?

3. How does Brian explain what Facebook is?

4. What does Mr Fitzgerald think about social networking sites?

5. What is Brian's opinion of social networking sites?

6. What is the danger of social networking sites in Mr Fitzgerald's opinion?

7. How many online friends has Sarah got?

8. Who is Sarah hoping to meet through Facebook?

9. What, in Mr Fitzgerald's opinion, is the advantage of books?

10. How many hours does Sarah usually spend on the computer?

2 Discussing social networking sites

___/16

a) Listen to the conversation again. Write down arguments for and against social networking sites mentioned by Sarah, Brian and Mr Fitzgerald. (6P)

Pros (+)	Cons (–)

b) What is your opinion? Add at least **two** of your own arguments to the table. (2P)

c) How social are social networking sites? Write a short comment of about **100** words. (8P)

_____
_____
_____
_____
_____
_____
_____
_____
_____
_____
_____

Unit 4 | Klassenarbeit A

LANGUAGE ____/47

1 WORDS You're beautiful, it's true ____/6

Complete the sentences with the correct translation of the German word "schön".

1 Your grandmother always told us what a _____ man your grandfather was when he was young.

2 Oh, such a _____ baby! How old is she?

3 I think you're the most _____ woman I've ever met.

4 Corsica is a _____ place to visit in spring.

5 Jim's _____, but he knows it and, if you ask me, that doesn't make him so _____.

2 WORDS Looking for Mr Right ____/9

In the hope of finding a nice boyfriend, Sarah has posted her profile in an online forum. Complete the text with **new words from Unit 4**.

Hi there,

My name is Sarah and I'm talking to all those _____ boys out there!

I don't like _____, so I'm going to _____ my thoughts

and tell you a bit about myself in a short text. I'm sixteen and still go to school. In my free time I

do some _____ work. I help old people with their shopping.

I don't mind being single because I've got really great

friends, but _____ I'm looking

for a _____. Only write to me if

you're serious and looking for a girlfriend. I don't want

a boyfriend who will _____

me or _____ me after a few weeks!

If you think you might be interested, then

_____ – as a tip I love pizza.

Looking forward to your reply.
Love, Sarah

3 GRAMMAR If we were a bit more careful, …

___ / 21

First write the tenses of the if-clauses (1–8) and the main clauses (A–H) into the table.
Then match the correct main clauses to the if-clauses. (16P)

If-Sätze – Conditional sentences (type 1, 2 and 3)

	If-clause	Main clause
Type 1: possible condition	simple present If I **go** to London,	– will-future – can/should/must + infinitive I **will visit** Buckingham Palace.
Type 2: improbable condition	simple past If my sister **went** to Australia,	– would/could/might + infinitive she **would visit** Sydney.
Type 3: impossible condition	past perfect If my uncle **hadn't moved** to New York,	– would/could/might + have + past participle he **would have come** to my birthday party.

Diese Tabelle hilft dir bei der Vervollständigung der Sätze. Überlege bei jedem Satz, welche Zeit im ersten Teil der Sätze 1–8 verwendet wird. Du kannst dann in der Tabelle oben die entsprechende Zeit ablesen. Wenn du dich sicher fühlst, deckst du die Tabelle oben einfach ab und kontrollierst anschließend.

1 If you upload that awful picture, _____

2 If everyone thought more about internet safety, _____

3 If our teacher hadn't explained how to use Facebook so patiently, _____

4 If my sister shops online tomorrow, _____

5 If Jane hadn't written so much about herself in the chatroom, _____

6 If I have time to use the computer today, _____

7 If dad let me surf the internet for a few hours every week, _____

8 If John hadn't been so rude in the chatroom, _____

A I will look for my friends on SchülerVZ. _____

B he could have taken part in the online discussion. _____

C she will order a new pair of shoes. _____

D everybody will be able to see it. _____

E we wouldn't have understood the possible problems. _____

F she wouldn't have met those awful guys. _____

G there wouldn't be as many dangers anymore. _____

H I could make a lot of new friends. _____

1	2	3	4	5	6	7	8

Now you

Complete the following sentences with suitable conditional endings. (5P)

1 If I didn't spend so much time talking to my neighbour during maths lessons, _____
   _____.

2 If Susan is able to save enough money, _____
   _____.

3 If Peter had understood the dangers of the internet, _____
   _____.

4 If the internet was more expensive, _____
   _____.

5 If our class decides to look for a partner school in England, _____
   _____.

4 GRAMMAR Giving advice _____/6

Complete the sentences with the correct translation of the German word "sollen".

> **German "sollen"**
> Für die Übersetzung des deutschen Wortes „sollen" gibt es im Englischen drei Möglichkeiten, die mit unterschiedlichen Bedeutungen verwendet werden:
> - **had better:** verwendest du in bestimmten Situationen, z. B: You'd better do the washing up before your mother comes home.
> - **should:** verwendest du in allgemeineren Situationen, z. B. You should listen to what your mother tells you.
> - **to be supposed to:** verwendest du, wenn du etwas zwar geplant hast, aber etwas anderes machst, z. B. I'm supposed to be going out tonight, but I don't really feel like it.

1 According to the website, the film _____ start at 8.30.

2 The auction ends in 20 minutes – you _____ decide if you need the CD or you'll miss it.

3 It's a great website, you really _____ visit it.

4 I _____ be doing my homework, but I really want to chat with my friends now.

5 It looks like it's going to be a difficult exam tomorrow – I _____ turn the computer off now.

6 If your computer is broken, you _____ buy a new one.

5 GRAMMAR Unusual road signs

___/5

Take a look at these road signs and write down what they mean.

Use **might**, **can**, **have to**, **must**, **should** and their negative forms. There may be more than one possible answer.

WRITING

____ / 20

Social networking sites – an essay

*You have been asked to write an **essay** for the school magazine about the pros and cons of Facebook and other social networking sites. In your text explain what social networking sites are, what you see as their benefits and what the possible negative aspects for users are. Write about **120** words.*

> **Argumentative writing**
> - Bei einem argumentativen Text solltest du vor dem Schreiben eine **Gliederung (Outline)** erstellen, mit der du deinen Text bereits in Einleitung, deine Argumente und Gegenargumente und Schlussgedanken strukturierst.
> - Denke beim Verfassen des Textes auch an **Beispiele**, die deine Meinung oder Auffassung unterstützen. Dies können – sofern vorhanden – auch Ergebnisse von Untersuchungen oder statistische Auswertungen sein. Zum **Schluss** deines Textes wiegst du Pro- und Contra-Argumente gegeneinander ab und ziehst eine persönliche Schlussfolgerung.
> - Weitere Tipps und Beispielgliederungen kannst du im Skills File auf S. 147 oder auf S. 82 in deinem Englischbuch nachlesen.

SPEAKING

___/17

🎧 10 Would you like to go out with me?

There is a new girl at school who has caught Peter's eye. He hasn't talked to her yet, but now she is sitting next to him on the bus and starts a conversation.

Listen to the conversation.

> ☞ Höre dir das Gespräch ein zweites Mal an und notiere dir nützliche Redewendungen. Sie helfen dir, wenn du dich in **Now you** selbst mit einer Mitschülerin oder einem Mitschüler verabredest. Falls du etwas nicht verstehst, höre dir den Abschnitt noch mal an.
> Wenn du mehr Hilfe benötigst, findest du den Hörtext bei den Lösungen.

🎧 11, 12 Now you: Asking a girl/boy out

There is a new girl/boy in your class who has caught your eye. You haven't talked to her/him yet, but now she/he is sitting next to you on the bus and starts a conversation.

Talk to her/him by pressing pause when you hear the beep.

> ☞ **Sprechen üben**
> ☐ Deine Audios findest du online auf scook.de. Gib dazu den Zugangscode von Seite 1 ein. Wähle Track 11 oder 12, je nachdem ob du dich mit einem Mädchen oder mit einem Jungen verabreden möchtest.
> ☐ Versuche, den Lückendialog möglichst frei zu sprechen.
> ☐ Wenn du noch Unterstützung benötigst, nimm deine Notizen zu Track 10 oder dein Englischbuch, S. 83 zur Hilfe.
> ☐ Du kannst deinen Dialog aufnehmen und dich so selbst kontrollieren oder Eltern und Freunde fragen.
> ☐ Vergleiche erst zum Schluss deine Lösung mit der Musterlösung.

Klassenarbeit B

Unit 4

Gesamtpunktzahl _____ / 70   Note _____

READING

_____ / 15

Bono: a celebrity campaigner

1 Hardly any rock star does as much to fight extreme poverty and hunger as the lead singer of the Irish band U2, Bono. Bono cannot accept that, there are countries where people have more money and more to eat than they could ever need, but at the same time there are people in other countries dying of hunger and disease.

2 Bono has said that he became interested in charity work when he watched one of the Secret Policeman's Balls, a charity show organized to raise money for the human rights organization Amnesty International. The first one took place in 1979 with famous comedians and musicians performing on the show for free. In 1986 Bono performed with U2 on an Amnesty International tour of the United States alongside Sting and Bryan Adams. Before that, in 1984, he took part in Bob Geldof's Band Aid project. Band Aid was a group of singers and musicians who raised money for victims of famine by selling a Christmas single called "Do they know it's Christmas?". The project was a huge success.

3 In 1985 Bono and U2 took part in the Live Aid concerts organized by Bob Geldof to raise more money for starving people in Ethiopia. Not long after that Bono and his wife went to Ethiopia to work in an orphanage for several weeks. In the mid-1980s Ethiopia was affected by a serious famine and poverty. The experience shocked Bono and made him determined to work to change the world.

4 Many of U2's songs have political messages, such as the song "Silver and Gold", the B-side to "Where the Streets Have no Name", which was written to support the "Artists United Against Apartheid" project. But besides his music, Bono has used his superstar status to put pressure on political leaders and to encourage them to change policy. For example at the G8 summit in 2005 he and Bob Geldof were allowed to meet US President George W. Bush and the German Chancellor Gerhard Schröder to talk to them about cancelling Third World debt and providing more financial support to Africa. In 2002 he also helped to create DATA, an organization which worked towards a fairer deal for Africa, as well as EDUN, a clothing company, which seeks to encourage trade with Africa. More recently he has founded ONE, an organization which fights extreme poverty and disease.

5 Bono has been nominated for the Nobel Peace Prize, was knighted by the Queen in 2007 and, with Bill and Melinda Gates, was one of TIME magazine's Persons of the Year in 2009.

1 Missing headings

_____ / 5

Match the headings A–E to paragraphs 1–5 of the article.

- **A** Awards for his work
- **B** More than just music
- **C** How Bono's campaign work started
- **D** Believe that you can change the world
- **E** A visit to Africa

1	2	3	4	5

Unit 4 | Klassenarbeit B

2 About the text ___ / 10

a) What examples are there in the text of Bono's campaign work? Make notes about at least **five** things. (5P)

_____
_____
_____
_____
_____
_____

b) Write about **50** words describing how Bono's campaign work began. (5P)

_____
_____
_____
_____
_____

LANGUAGE ___ / 37

1 WORDS A network ___ / 7

a) Complete the **network** about charity work. (3P)

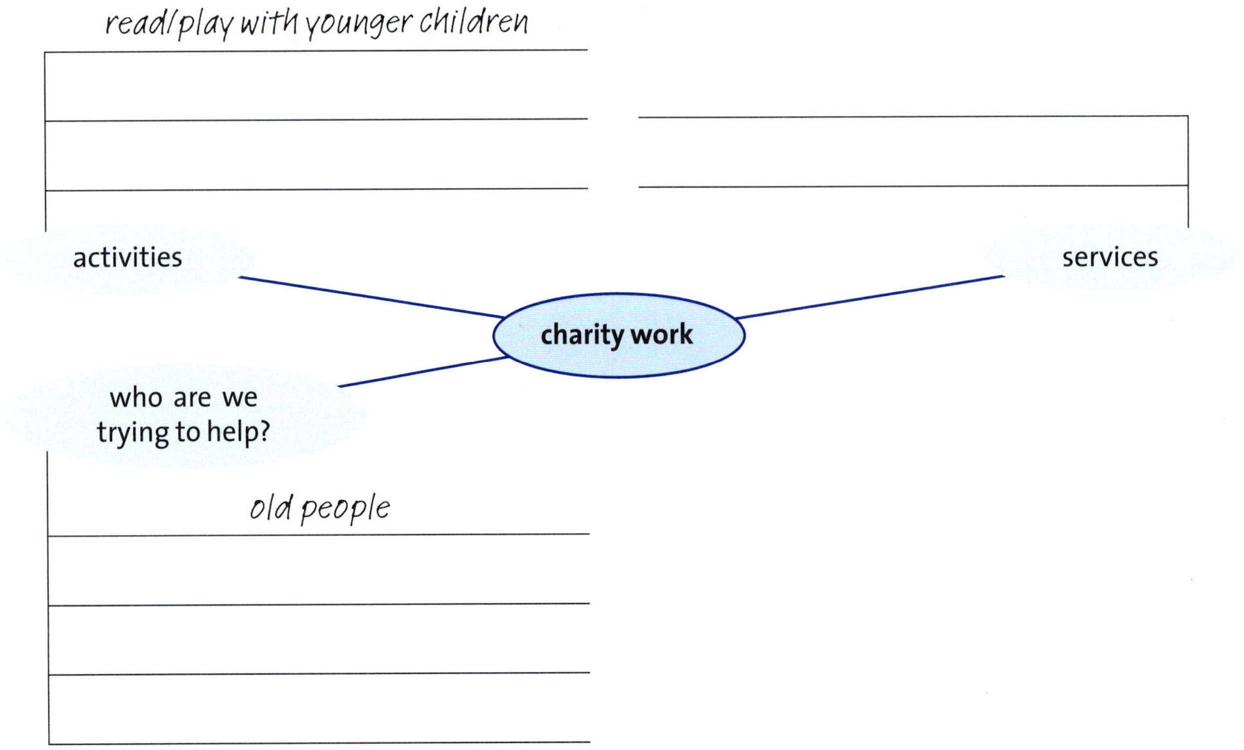

read/play with younger children

- activities
- services
- **charity work**
- who are we trying to help?
- *old people*

© 2011 Cornelsen Verlag, Berlin. Alle Rechte vorbehalten.

b) *Josh is a member of the Scouts in the United States. His group does a lot for the environment and for people in need.*

In the following sentences he tells you about the kind of work the Scouts do. Complete the text with words from the network in **a)**. *(3P)*

With the Scouts we regularly do _____.

One of the things we do every week is _____.

The last time we went out we found an old fridge which someone had just left in the woods. And guess what, it still worked!

So we cleaned it up and sold it at a flea market. We decided to _____ the money we got to the local _____ which provides _____ and homeless people with a warm meal, so that they don't go _____.

2 WORDS Using new words ____/7

Complete the text with words from **Unit 4**.

1. I was playing with my mobile phone as I was walking down the street and I _____ a lamppost. How embarrassing!

2. Laura _____. She delivers newspapers to the people in my street.

3. Peter likes animals. Yesterday I saw him _____ his neighbour's _____.

4. David's such a _____. He's so polite and always thinks of other people.

5. Gosh, there is a long queue. We'll have to be _____.

6. Don't _____ to like mathematics. I know you hate it!

7. I don't go out after dark. I'm afraid of _____.

3 GRAMMAR Some might say …   ___/4

*Liza is talking about her charity work. Make the sentences shorter by using **the + adjective**.*

1 Our charity work helps people who are very poor.
   Our charity work helps the poor.

2 At our school there should be elevators for students who cannot walk.
   _____

3 Young people go out more than old people (2x).
   _____

4 I raise money to help people who have no home.
   _____

5 Sometimes I feel like Robin Hood, when I take money from people who are rich and give it to poor people (2x).
   _____

4 GRAMMAR Liza's birthday party   ___/7

Liza recently celebrated her 15th birthday. Here she is describing the start of her day.

Choose words from the box and use the correct forms (adjective or adverb) to complete the text.

> careful • delicious • exciting • fantastic •
> hungry • impatient • slow

 Denke daran, dass nach Verben der Wahrnehmung (z. B. **look, sound, smell, taste, feel**) stets ein Adjektiv steht!

I woke up to the _____ smell of a cake baking, which had filled the whole house. It might not sound particularly _____ to you, but my mum bakes incredible cakes. I went _____ downstairs and listened _____ for sounds from the kitchen. I looked through the door and saw my mum standing _____ in front of the oven door. I knew she wanted the cake to be ready before I got up. She took the _____ looking cake out of the oven and, as we were both feeling _____, we ate two pieces straight away!

5 GRAMMAR An incredible trip

____ / 6

This summer Sam and Luke stayed with a Spanish host family. During their stay, there were some things they had to do and other things which they were allowed to do.

Make complete sentences from the notes using **make** or **let** + **object** + **infinitive**.

1 Clean room ourselves – once a week
2 Stay out until 2 in the morning
3 Use private TV and PC – any time
4 Eat fish or meat – every day
5 Pay €50 extra – day trips
6 Look after baby José – one hour every day

1 _____
2 _____
3 _____
4 _____
5 _____
6 _____

6 GRAMMAR The Scout hut

___/6

Josh and the Boy Scouts have recently moved into a new Scout hut. To get the place ready for their first meeting, they had to prepare a lot of things. The Scouts did many of the jobs themselves, but some had to be done by other people.

*Look at the pictures and write sentences using **have** + **object** + **past participle** where suitable.*

1 _____

2 _____

3 _____

4 _____

5 _____

6 _____

Unit 4 | Klassenarbeit B

MEDIATION

___/ 18

Doing community service

Ahmed is an exchange student at your school. He would like to stay in Germany to do some voluntary community service when he has finished his exchange year. He has done some research about the "Freiwilliges Soziales Jahr", which is open to foreign students if they speak German. However, he doesn't really understand the details of this text from Hesse and needs your help.

*Read the website, then **summarize** the text in an e-mail to Ahmed.*

FSJ in Hessen

Viele junge Menschen betreuen Kinder oder hilfebedürftige Menschen und es macht ihnen Spaß. Gehören Sie auch dazu? Oder haben Sie vielleicht schon darüber nachgedacht, wo Sie sich sozial engagieren könnten?

Das Freiwillige Soziale Jahr – FSJ – ist eine solche Möglichkeit. Es bietet jungen Menschen die Chance, bei der Erziehung von Kindern oder der Betreuung von alten und kranken Menschen oder Menschen mit Behinderungen mitzuhelfen – durch persönliche Unterstützung, Begleitung oder Zuwendung. Die jungen Menschen sammeln Erfahrungen, die sie sowohl für den späteren Beruf als auch für das Zusammenleben prägen. Das FSJ ist ein Angebot, das mehr als eine Überlegung wert ist.

Ein Jahr können sich freiwillige Helferinnen und Helfer zwischen 16 und 27 Jahren in einer sozialen, sportlichen oder kulturellen Einrichtung engagieren. Die Einsatzorte reichen von Krankenhäusern über Altenheime bis zu kulturellen und sportlichen Organisationen oder Einrichtungen für Kinder und Jugendliche. Die FSJ-Helferinnen und FSJ-Helfer können sich in Hessen und im Ausland einbringen. Mit dem FSJ kann die Zeit zwischen Schule und Beruf gefüllt werden.

Die FSJ-Helferinnen und FSJ-Helfer bekommen für ihren Einsatz ein Taschengeld, Verpflegung und Unterkunft. Informationen zum FSJ in Hessen sind im Internet unter www.fsj-hessen.de abrufbar. Hier werden alle hessischen FSJ Träger im Kurzprofil vorgestellt – von der Arbeiterwohlfahrt bis zur Katholischen Kirche. So lässt sich schnell feststellen, in welchem Bereich und an welchen Orten man als FSJ-Helferin oder FSJ-Helfer bei den einzelnen Trägern tätig werden möchte. Außerdem findet man hier alle wichtigen Kontaktadressen und Ansprechpartnerinnen und -partner.

How to do well in a test

Countdown zum Testerfolg

Ein Test ist angekündigt? Kein Grund zur Panik. Wichtig ist, dass du weißt, worauf du dich vorbereiten musst. Im Zweifelsfall frag deine Lehrerin oder deinen Lehrer. Der Countdown kann beginnen!

Eine Woche vor dem Test

1. Lies noch einmal die **Texte** der zuletzt durchgenommenen Unit (A-Section und Text, eventuell auch das Background File). Fasse mündlich oder schriftlich zusammen, worum es ging.
2. Wiederhole den **Wortschatz** der Unit mit Hilfe des *Vocabulary* oder des *Wordmaster*. Schreibe dir die Wörter und Wortverbindungen, die du immer wieder vergisst, auf ein Blatt Papier. Eine Mindmap oder ein Wortfeld helfen beim Behalten.
3. Geh auch noch mal die neue **Grammatik** durch. Aufgaben zur Selbstüberprüfung und zum Üben findest du im *Practice*-Teil, auf der Seite „How am I doing?", im *Grammar File* (S. 153–180), in deinem *Workbook* und im *e-Workbook*.

Zwei Tage vor dem Test

1. Wiederhole den **Wortschatz**. Manche Wörter sitzen noch nicht? Schreibe einen kurzen Text, in dem du sie verwendest.
2. Lies die **Texte** ein weiteres Mal.
3. Erkläre einem Freund oder einer Freundin die neue **Grammatik**. Das klappt nicht richtig? Dann lies nochmal im *Grammar File* nach.

Am Abend vor dem Test

1. Entspanne dich. Du kannst lesen, dich in die Badewanne legen, Musik hören, fernsehen, …
2. Geh zur gewohnten Zeit ins Bett.

Am Morgen des Tests

1. Steh rechtzeitig auf, damit du nicht hetzen musst.
2. Lies irgendetwas „zum Aufwärmen", aber schau nicht mehr in dein Schülerbuch.

Während des Tests

1. Denk daran: Du hast dich gut vorbereitet. Es gibt keinen Grund, nervös zu sein.
2. Konzentriere dich auf den Test, lass dich nicht ablenken.
3. Lies dir die Aufgaben genau durch. Dann löse zuerst die Aufgaben, die dir einfach scheinen. Wende dich erst danach den schwereren Aufgaben zu.
4. Aufgaben, die du bearbeitet hast, hakst du ab. So siehst du, wie du vorankommst, und behältst den Überblick.
5. Schau ab und zu auf die Uhr. Du solltest dir für den Schluss noch etwas Zeit einplanen, um deine Antworten noch einmal durchzulesen und wenn nötig zu korrigieren.

Aufgabenstellungen verstehen

Bevor du anfängst, die Aufgaben zu bearbeiten, vergewissere dich, dass du genau weißt, was du tun sollst. Lies die Aufgabe Wort für Wort langsam und gründlich und von Anfang bis Ende durch. Du kannst besonders wichtige Teile der Aufgabenstellung unterstreichen und die Aufgabe, wenn nötig, für dich in einzelne Schritte unterteilen.

Den folgenden Arbeitsanweisungen begegnest du häufig:

Add	Verbinde eine Information oder einen Sachverhalt mit einer/einem anderen auf die geforderte Art und Weise.
Choose	Wähle zwischen verschiedenen Möglichkeiten die passende Information aus.
Comment	Kommentiere einen Sachverhalt durch die Darstellung deiner eigenen Meinung dazu. Begründe und erläutere sie möglichst genau.
Compare	Vergleiche Dinge, Wörter oder Sachverhalte, indem du prüfst, ob und auf welche Weise sie gleiche oder verschiedene Eigenschaften, Aussehen, Bedeutungen oder Funktionen haben.
Complete	Ergänze eine Information, indem du sie an dem dafür vorgesehenen Platz einträgst und damit z. B. einen Satz sinnvoll beendest.
Describe	Beschreibe ein Objekt oder eine Person, d.h. stelle dar, wie sie aussehen, wie das Objekt funktioniert oder die Personen handeln. Vermeide eigene Wertungen wie z. B. „beautiful", „useful" oder „great".
Discuss	Diskutiere ein Thema, eine Behauptung oder eine Aussage. Untersuche möglichst viele Seiten davon, z. B. Vor- und Nachteile, und stelle diese geordnet dar.
Explain	Erkläre einen Sachverhalt, d. h. gib wesentliche Fakten über ihn und erläutere, wie sie logisch zusammenhängen.
Fill in	Trage die geforderten Informationen in den dafür vorgesehenen Platz ein, z. B. in eine Lücke oder eine Tabelle.
List	Schreibe einzelne oder mehrere Informationen übersichtlich und geordnet auf, z. B. in einer Reihe, Tabelle oder einem anderen Verzeichnis.
Listen	Höre dir einen Text, einzelne Informationen oder Sachverhalte an.
Match	Ordne die angegebenen Informationen einander zu, wie es die Aufgabe erfordert. Finde z. B. Satzanfänge und passende Satzenden und füge sie zusammen.
Use	Verwende eine Tatsache, ein Wort usw. so, wie es in der Aufgabe gefordert wird.
Write a ...	Schreibe etwas in einem geforderten Textformat auf, z. B. deinen Kommentar zu etwas oder eine Geschichte.